SNOOPY STARS

STARS

— AS —

THE MATCHMAKER

Charles M. Schulz

RAVETTE BOOKS

This edition first published by
Ravette Books Limited 1988

Printed and bound in Great Britain
for Ravette Books Limited,
3 Glenside Estate, Star Road, Partridge Green,
Horsham, Sussex RH13 8RA
by Cox & Wyman Ltd, Reading

ISBN 1 85304 027 4

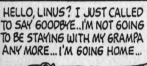

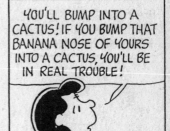

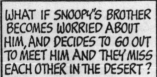

PEANUTS

I'VE BEEN WONDERING ABOUT SOMETHING

I'VE BEEN WONDERING IF YOU EVER MET THAT CUTE LITTLE COYOTE THAT SPIKE TOLD YOU ABOUT...

I MET HER ALL RIGHT, AND SHE WAS THE CUTEST LITTLE THING I'VE EVER SEEN...BUT WE HAD STRONG RELIGIOUS DIFFERENCES...

12-3

SHE ATE BUNNIES!

PEANUTS

Napoleon was ready to leave for Moscow.

He kissed his wife, and whispered farewell.

11-30

As he rode off to battle, she shouted, "Don't get blown apart, Bonapart!"

WELL, SHE MIGHT HAVE SAID IT!

"You didn't keep your promise," she said.

7-9

"When I married you, you said we'd live in a vine covered cottage."

"All right! All right!" he shouted

© 1977 United Feature Syndicate, Inc.

"You go talk to the Planning Commission!"

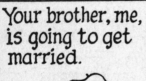

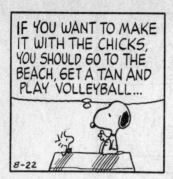

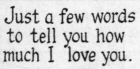

Dear Valentine,

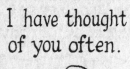

I have thought of you often.

2-8

© 1983 United Feature Syndicate, Inc.

Not all the time, but often.

Dear Sweetheart,
Without you my
days are endless.

Days seem like
weeks...weeks like
months...

Months like years...
Years like centuries..
Centuries like...

You get the idea.

© 1983 United Feature Syndicate, Inc

SCHULZ

1-3-84

Dear Sweetheart,
I think of you
night and day.

5-3

You are more precious
to me than anything
in the world.

SUPPERTIME!

© 1984 United Feature Syndicate, Inc.

SCHULZ

EVERY DAY I LOOK FORWARD TO SEEING THAT BEAUTIFUL GIRL DRIVE BY HERE IN HER PICKUP...

I'M ALWAYS AFRAID SHE'LL GET TIRED OF WAVING TO ME...

10-27

MAYBE I COULD DO SOMETHING UNUSUAL TO MAKE HER LAUGH...

HIPPITY-
HOP

BUNNIES HIPPITY-HOP...
DOGS DON'T HIPPITY-HOP..

1-21

Other Snoopy titles published by Ravette Books

Snoopy Stars in this series
No. 1	Snoopy Stars as The Flying Ace	£1.95
No. 3	Snoopy Stars as The Terror of the Ice	£1.95
No. 4	Snoopy Stars as The Legal Beagle	£1.95
No. 5	Snoopy Stars as The Fearless Leader	£1.95
No. 6	Snoopy Stars as Man's Best Friend	£1.95

Colour landscapes
First Serve	£2.95
Be Prepared	£2.95
Stay Cool	£2.95
Shall We Dance?	£2.95
Let's Go	£2.95
Come Fly With Me	£2.95

Black and white landscapes
It's a Dog's Life	£2.50
Roundup	£2.50
Freewheelin'	£2.50
Joe Cool	£2.50
Dogs Don't Eat Dessert	£2.50
You're on the Wrong Foot Again, Charlie Brown	£2.50

All these books are available at your local bookshop or news-agent, or can be ordered direct from the publisher. Just tick the titles you require and fill in the form below. Prices and availability subject to change without notice.

Ravette Books Limited, 3 Glenside Estate, Star Road, Partridge Green, Horsham, West Sussex RH13 8RA

Please send a cheque or postal order, and allow the following for postage and packing. UK: 45p for one book plus 30p for each additional book.

Name ....

Address ....

....